VEHICLES

MOTORCYCLES

Written by Bethany Latham

Genius Kid

This edition is published by arrangement with BookLife Publishing

sales@northstareditions.com | 888-417-0195

Library of Congress Control Number:
2025943953

ISBN
979-8-89471-067-9 (library bound)
979-8-89471-087-7 (paperback)
979-8-89471-123-2 (epub)
979-8-89471-107-2 (hosted ebook)

Printed in the United States of America
Mankato, MN
012026

Written by:
Bethany Latham

Edited by:
Rebecca Phillips-Bartlett

Designed by:
Ker Ker Lee

Photo Credits – Images courtesy of Shutterstock.com, unless otherwise stated.

Cover – MiloVad, ParinPix, Theeradech Sanin, Luis Louro, Oleksandr Grechin, BEST-BACKGROUNDS, LIAL, Viktor Vy, Pixe1Power, athanop_night, Cara Kate. 2–3 – Kittipong33, Lukas Gojda, Dani Jazmi. 4–5 – hayricaliskan, Jakub Sisulak, New Africa. 6–7 – Kasefoto, vladancipi, Kulikou Siarhei, Inc. 8–9 – lennystan, Armensl, ricochet64, Wozzie, New Africa, sylv1rob1, Michael Dechevl. 10–11 – Maria Markevich, Dani Jazmi, muroPhotographer, Pixe1Power, Jakub Sisulak. 12–13 – arda savasciogullari. 14–15 – kikk, Alexandru Nika, sugarajfm, chanonnat srisura, Winai Tepsuttinun. 16–17 – Panos Karas, VectorMine. 18–19 – putrakurniawan78, Cornelius Krishna Tedjo, Thomas Dutour, Vlad Linev, Veronica Louro. 20–21 – B.Forenius, Porstocker, JHVEPhoto, Bertrandbat. 22–23 – diametrix, Porstocker, Krakenimages.com, LIAL, Sergey Ryzhov.

CONTENTS

Page 4	Motorcycles
Page 6	Key Words
Page 8	A Timeline of Motorcycles
Page 10	Types of Motorcycles
Page 12	Motorcycle Parts
Page 14	In the Rider's Seat
Page 16	Inside the Engine
Page 18	Safety First
Page 20	Believe It or Not!
Page 22	Are You a Genius Kid?
Page 24	Glossary and Index

Words that look like this can be found in the glossary on page 24.

MOTORCYCLES

Have you ever seen someone riding a motorcycle?

Motorcycles are vehicles. They can carry one or two people.

Motorcycles have engines and two wheels.

Motorcycles look like bicycles. However, motorcycles are bigger, heavier, and faster.

Riding motorcycles comes with a little more risk than driving other vehicles. It's important that they are used safely.

KEY WORDS

Here are some key words about motorcycles that every genius kid should learn.

MOTORCYCLIST

A motorcyclist is someone who rides a motorcycle. Motorcyclists are also called riders.

HELMET

Helmets protect motorcyclists' heads while they are driving.

ARMOR

Armor is the protective padding motorcyclists wear. It keeps their bodies safe. Full armor often includes knee pads and gloves. Armor is also called leathers.

MOTOCROSS

Motocross is the sport of off-road motorcycle racing.

A TIMELINE OF MOTORCYCLES

Around 1867

Sylvester H. Roper built a steam-powered bicycle.

1901–1903

Many famous motorcycle companies were created, including Harley-Davidson.

1885

Gottlieb Daimler and Wilhelm Maybach built the first motorcycle with a combustion engine.

1907

The first Isle of Man Tourist Trophy motorcycle race took place. It is now one of the world's most famous motorcycle races.

1974

Mike Corbin set a record for the fastest speed traveled on an electric motorcycle at 165 mph (265.5 kph).

2006

The first motorcycles with airbags were sold.

Now

There are more than 100 motorcycle makers in the world.

TYPES OF MOTORCYCLES

There are many different types of motorcycles.

Mopeds are small motorcycles. They usually have a top speed of around 30 miles (48 km) per hour.

Moped

Scooter

Scooters have small wheels. They have a floorboard that riders rest their feet on. They are often used for city travel.

Dirt bikes are driven on rough ground. They are light and fast and have bumpy tires.

Dirt bike

Cruiser

Cruisers are big motorcycles with low seats.

Sport motorcycle

Sport motorcycles are built for speed. They are used for racing.

MOTORCYCLE PARTS

On the outside, most motorcycles have similar parts.

The exhaust is where gas from the engine comes out.

The footpegs are what motorcyclists rest their feet on.

The handlebars are used to steer the motorcycle.

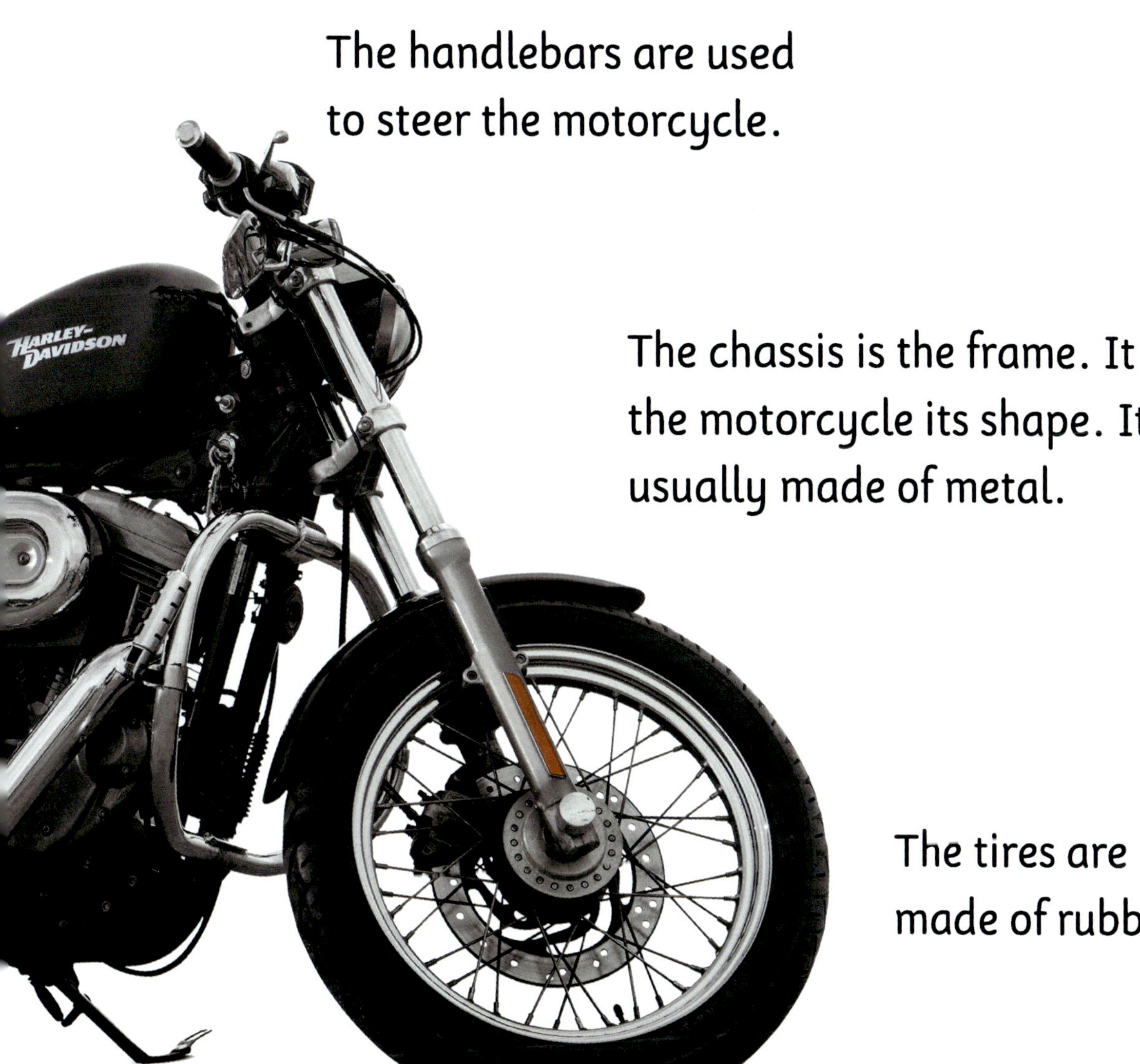

The chassis is the frame. It gives the motorcycle its shape. It is usually made of metal.

The tires are made of rubber.

IN THE RIDER'S SEAT

Motorcycles have many parts that help them work.

The throttle is on the handlebars. The rider twists the throttle to control the motorcycle's speed.

Throttle

Brake lever

The brake lever is on the right handlebar. It controls the front brakes.

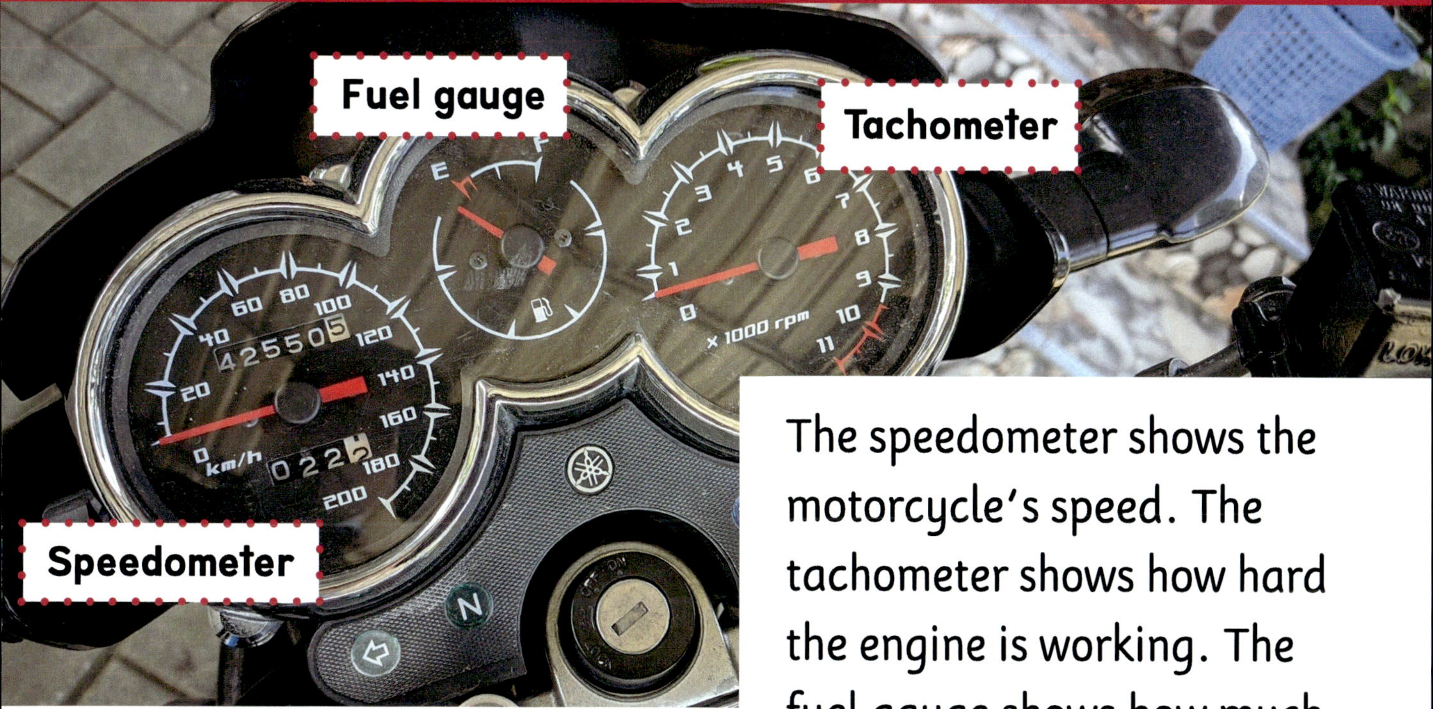

Fuel gauge

Tachometer

Speedometer

The speedometer shows the motorcycle's speed. The tachometer shows how hard the engine is working. The fuel gauge shows how much fuel the motorcycle has.

The rider changes gears with the gear shift lever.

Gear shift lever

The rear brake pedal controls the motorcycle's back brake.

Rear brake pedal

INSIDE THE ENGINE

Like cars, most motorcycles have internal combustion engines. Combustion engines usually use gasoline as fuel. Gasoline is a liquid mixture made from petroleum.

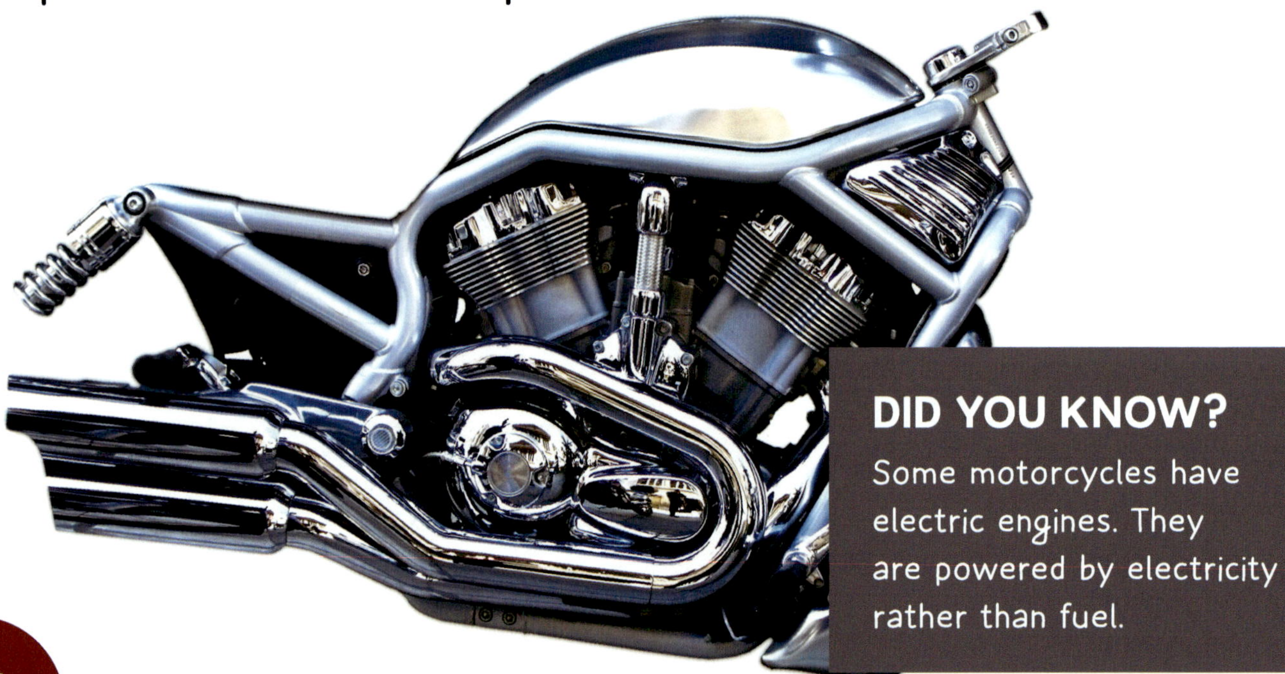

DID YOU KNOW?

Some motorcycles have electric engines. They are powered by electricity rather than fuel.

Air and fuel are pulled into the engine.

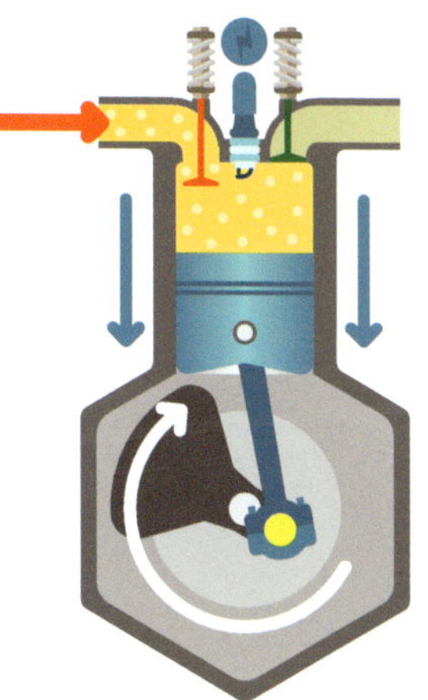

They are then squeezed and ignited with a spark.

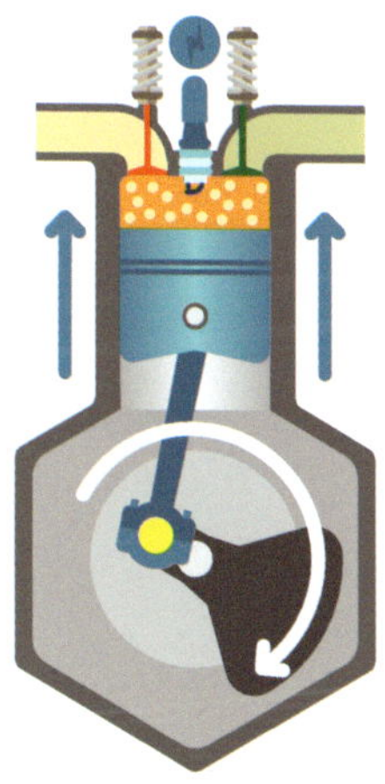

The spark creates a small explosion inside the engine.

The explosion creates gas that makes engine parts called pistons go up and down. This makes the motorcycle go.

SAFETY FIRST

There are many things on a motorcycle that keep the rider safe.

The horn tells other people the motorcycle is there.

Headlights help the rider see at night. Turning signals tell other people which direction the motorcycle is turning.

Mudguards sit over the wheels. They protect the rider and motorcycle from dirt and debris coming off the road.

Brakes allow the motorcycle to stop.

BELIEVE IT OR NOT!

Yamaha is a Japanese motorcycle company. But it started off making musical instruments! The company made its first motorcycle in 1955.

Royal Enfield is the oldest motorcycle maker in the world. The company began in 1901.

The longest motorcycle in the world is more than 85 feet (26 m) long. It was made by Bharat Sinh Parmar in 2014.

Elspeth Beard was the first British woman to ride a motorcycle around the world. Her journey started in 1982. It ended in 1984.

ARE YOU A GENIUS KID?

You have learned many awesome motorcycle facts to wow your friends and family with. But first, it's time to test your knowledge. Are you really a genius kid?

Check back through the book if you are not sure.

1. How many motorcycle makers are there in the world today?
2. What is the name of the motorcycle's frame?
3. In what year did Elspeth Beard begin her motorcycle journey around the world?

Answers:
1. more than 100
2. chassis
3. 1982

GLOSSARY

airbags safety cushions that inflate quickly during a crash and protect the passenger's body

combustion engine an engine that is powered by burning or setting fire to something

debris loose pieces of something that has broken

fuel something that can be used to make energy or power something

gears parts of a machine that make other parts move; different gears help motorcycles move at different speeds

ignited made to catch fire or explode

vehicles machines that are used to carry people or things

INDEX

bicycles 5, 8
brakes 14–15, 19
engines 4, 8, 12, 15–17
fuel 15–17
handlebars 13–14
helmets 6
leathers 7
motorcyclists 6–7, 12
riders 6, 10, 14–15, 18–19
wheels 4, 10, 19